Give It *All* to *Him*

Give It All to Him

A Story of New Beginnings

Max Lucado

Thomas Nelson
Since 1798

NASHVILLE DALLAS MEXICO CITY RIO DE JANEIRO BEIJING

Compiled by Troy Schmidt.

Published by W Publishing Group, a Division of Thomas Nelson, Inc., P.O. Box 141000, Nashville, Tennessee 37214.

All Scripture quotations, unless otherwise indicated, are taken from The Holy Bible, New International Version. Copyright © 1973, 1978, 1984, International Bible Society. Used by permission of Zondervan Bible Publishers. Other Scripture references are from the following sources: The Contemporary English Version (CEV) © 1991 by the American Bible Society. Used by permission. The King James Version of the Bible (KJV). The Message (MSG), copyright © 1993. Used by permission of NavPress Publishing Group. New American Standard Bible (NASB), © 1960, 1977, 1995 by the Lockman Foundation. The New Century Version® (NCV). Copyright © 1987, 1988, 1991 by Word Publishing, a Division of Thomas Nelson, Inc. Used by permission. All rights reserved. The New King James Version (NKJV®), copyright 1979, 1980, 1982, Thomas Nelson, Inc., Publishers. The Holy Bible, New Living Translation (NLT), copyright © 1996. Used by permission of Tyndale House Publishers, Inc., Wheaton, Illinois 60189. All rights reserved. J. B. Phillips: The New Testament in Modern English, Revised Edition (PHILLIPS). Copyright © J. B. Phillips 1958, 1960, 1972. Used by permission of Macmillan Publishing Co., Inc.

Library of Congress Cataloging-in-Publication Data

Lucado, Max.
    Give it all to Him / by Max Lucado.
       p. cm.
    Includes bibliographical references.

    ISBN-13: 978-0-8499-4478-9
    1. Conversion—Christianity. I. Title.
BV4921.3.L83 2004
242—dc22   2003024237

Printed in the United States of America

15 14 13 12 11 OPM 25 24 23 22

CONTENTS

CARRYING
THE WEIGHT

The woman flops down on the bench and drops her trash bag between her feet. With elbows on knees and cheeks in hands, she stares at the sidewalk. Everything aches. Back. Legs. Neck. Her shoulder is stiff and her hands raw. All because of the sack.

Oh, to be rid of this garbage.

Unbroken clouds form a gray ceiling, gray with a thousand sorrows. Soot-stained buildings cast long shadows, darkening passageways and the people in them. Drizzle chills the air and muddies the rivulets of the street gutters. The woman collects her jacket. A passing car drenches the sack and splashes her jeans. She doesn't move. Too tired.

Her memories of life without the trash are fuzzy. As a child maybe? Her back was straighter, her walk quicker . . . or was it a dream? She doesn't know for sure.

A second car. This one stops and parks. A man steps out. She watches his shoes sink in the slush. From the car he pulls out a trash bag, lumpy with litter. He drapes it over his shoulder and curses the weight.

Neither of them speaks. Who knows if he noticed her. His face seems young, younger than his stooped back. In moments he is gone. Her gaze returns to the pavement.

She never looks at her trash. Early on she did. But what she saw repulsed her, so she's kept the sack closed ever since.

What else can she do? Give it to someone? All have their own.[1]

Suddenly one day we notice that our step has lost its spring. The sky has lost its blue. Our memory book has faded, its pictures yellowed and blurry. We didn't plan for this. It just happened.

That's when we look down and notice something in our hands. A trash bag filled to capacity. Or maybe two, both of them bulky and cumbersome. Who handed us this? How did we get it? And how do we get rid of it?

You don't find bags of trash selling well on eBay. Nobody wants garbage. We all have plenty in our own lives, and we, too, are trying to find ways of getting rid of it.

You may not understand where the load came from or what to do with it, but you know one thing—carrying all this junk around can't be good for you.

The *Pelicano* is the world's most unwanted ship. Since 1986 she has been the hobo of the high seas. No one wants her. Sri Lanka doesn't. Bermuda doesn't. The Dominican Republic turned her away. So did the Netherlands, the Antilles, and Honduras.

The problem is not the boat. Though rusty and barnacled, the 466-foot freighter is seaworthy.

The problem is not the ownership. The owners have kept the license current and taxes paid.

The problem is not the crew. They may feel unwanted, but they aren't inefficient.

Then what is the problem? What is the reason for years of rejections? Waved away in Sri Lanka. Turned away in Indonesia. Rejected in Haiti. Why is the *Pelicano* the most unwanted ship in the world?

Simple. She is full of trash. Fifteen thousand tons of trash. Orange peelings. Beer bottles. Newspapers. Half-eaten hot dogs. Trash. The trash of Philadelphia's long summer of 1986. That's when the municipal workers went on strike. That's when the trash piled higher and higher. That's when

Georgia refused it and New Jersey declined it. No one wanted Philadelphia's trash.

That's when the *Pelicano* entered the picture. The owners thought they would turn a quick penny by transporting the rubbish. The trash was burned, and the ashes were dumped into the belly of the boat. But no one would take it. Initially it was too much. Eventually it was too old. Who wants potentially toxic trash?[2]

The plight of the *Pelicano* is proof. Trash-filled ships find few friends. The plight of the *Pelicano* is also a parable. Trash-filled hearts don't fare any better.

I wonder if you can relate to the *Pelicano*. Are you unwanted at the dock? Drifting farther from friends and family? If so, you might check your heart for garbage. Who wants to offer dock space to a smelly heart?

Life has a way of unloading her rubbish on our decks. Your husband works too much. Your wife gripes too much. Your boss expects too much. Your kids whine too much. The result? Trash. Load after load of anger. Guilt. Pessimism. Bitterness. Bigotry. Anxiety. Deceit. Impatience. It all piles up.

Trash affects us. It contaminates our relationships. It did Cain's. He had anger in his mind before he had blood on his hands. And Martha? Martha was meddlesome in her attitude before she was quarrelsome with her tongue. And what about the Pharisees? They killed Christ in their hearts before they killed him on the cross.[3]

Mark it down. Today's thoughts are tomorrow's actions.

Today's jealousy is tomorrow's temper tantrum.

Today's bigotry is tomorrow's hate crime.

Today's anger is tomorrow's abuse.

Today's lust is tomorrow's adultery.

Today's greed is tomorrow's embezzlement.

Today's guilt is tomorrow's fear.

Today's thoughts are tomorrow's actions. Could that be why Paul wrote, "Love . . . keeps no record of wrongs" (1 Cor. 13:4–5)? Let trash on board, and people are going to smell it. The troubles for the *Pelicano* began with the first shovelful. The crew should have turned it away at the gate. Life would have been easier for everyone on board if they had never allowed the trash to pile up.

Life will be better for you if you do the same. . . .

You can stick with your stinky cargo. And drift from port to port.

But why would you? Let the *Pelicano* have the high seas.

Your Captain has better plans for you.[4]

What's inside the Bags?

Here comes a young mother. With one hand she leads a child; with the other she drags her load, bumpy and heavy.

Here comes an old man, face ravined with wrinkles. His trash sack is so long it hits the back of his legs as he walks. He glances at the woman and tries to smile.

What weight would he be carrying? *she wonders as he passes.*

"Regrets."

She turns to see who spoke. Beside her on the bench sits a man. Tall, with angular cheeks and bright, kind eyes. Like hers, his jeans are mud stained. Unlike hers, his shoulders are straight. He wears a T-shirt and baseball cap. She looks around for his trash but doesn't see it.

He watches the old man disappear as he explains, "As a young father, he worked many hours and neglected his family. His children don't love him. His sack is full, full of regrets."

She doesn't respond. And when she doesn't, he does.

"And yours?"

"Mine?" she asks, looking at him.

"Shame." His voice is gentle, compassionate.

She still doesn't speak, but neither does she turn away.

"Too many hours in the wrong arms. Last year. Last night . . . shame."

Sifting through people's trash tells a lot about them. What kind of food they eat (are they health conscious or fast-food junkies?). What kind of reading materials they ingest. Their favorite soap (if they use any at all). Their private letters. Their discarded memories.

Look inside your trash bag. What is it that you need to throw out but for some reason just can't . . . or don't . . . or won't?

LONELINESS

Judy was not a prostitute. She was not on drugs or on welfare. She never went to jail. She was not a social outcast. She was respectable. She jogged. She hosted parties. She wore designer clothes and had an apartment that overlooked the bay. And she was very lonely. "I see people together and I'm so jealous I want to throw up. What about me? What about me?!" Though surrounded by people, she was on an island. Though she had many acquaintances, she had few friends. Though she had many lovers (fifty-nine in fifty-six months), she had little love.

"Who is going to love Judy Bucknell?" she wrote in her diary. "I feel so old. Unloved. Unwanted. Abandoned. Used up. I want to cry and sleep forever."[2]

A clear message came from her aching words. Though her body died on June 9 from the wounds of a knife, her heart had died long before. . . .

"I'm alone," she wrote, "and I want to share something with somebody."[3]

Loneliness.

It's a cry. A moan, a wail. It's a gasp whose origin is the recesses of our souls.

Can you hear it? The abandoned child. The divorcée. The quiet home. The empty mailbox. The long days. The longer nights. A one-night stand. A forgotten birthday. A silent phone . . .

Listen again. Tune out the traffic and turn down the TV. The cry is there. Our cities are full of Judy Bucknells. You can hear their cries. You can hear them in the convalescent home among the sighs and the shuffling feet. You can hear them in the prisons among the moans of shame and the calls for mercy. You can hear them if you walk the manicured streets of suburban America, among the aborted ambitions and aging homecoming queens. Listen for it in the halls of our high schools where peer pressure weeds out the "have-nots" from the "haves."

This moan in a minor key knows all spectrums of society. From the top to the bottom. From the failures to the famous. From the poor to the rich. From the married to the single. Judy Bucknell was not alone.[4]

WORRY

Worry is the burlap bag of burdens. It's overflowing with "whaddifs" and "howells." "Whaddif it rains at my wedding?" "Howell I know when to discipline my kids?" "Whaddif I marry a guy who snores?" "Howell we pay our baby's tuition?" "Whaddif, after all my dieting, they learn that lettuce is fattening and chocolate isn't?"

The burlap bag of worry. Cumbersome. Chunky. Unattractive. Scratchy. Hard to get a handle on. Irritating to carry and impossible to give away. No one wants your worries.

The truth be told, you don't want them either. No one has to remind you of the high cost of anxiety. (But I will anyway.) Worry divides the mind. The biblical word for *worry (merimnao)* is a compound of two Greek words, *merizo* ("to divide") and *nous* ("the mind"). Anxiety splits our energy between today's priorities and tomorrow's problems. Part of the mind is on the now; the rest is on the not yet. The result is half-minded living.

That's not the only result. Worrying is not a disease, but it causes diseases. It has been connected to high blood pressure, heart trouble, blindness, migraine headaches, thyroid malfunctions, and a host of stomach disorders.

Anxiety is an expensive habit. Of course, it might be worth the cost if it worked. But it doesn't. Our frets are futile. Jesus said, "You cannot add any time to your life by worrying about it" (Matt. 6:27 NCV). Worry has never brightened a day, solved a problem, or cured a disease.[5]

PAIN

Perhaps the wound is old. A parent abused you. A teacher slighted you. A mate betrayed you. A business partner bailed out, leaving you a choice of bills or bankruptcy.

And you are angry.

Or perhaps the wound is fresh. The friend who owes you money just drove by in a new car. The boss who hired you with promises of promotions has forgotten how to pronounce your name. Your circle of friends escaped on a weekend getaway, and you weren't invited. The children you raised seem to have forgotten you exist.

And you are hurt.

Part of you is broken, and the other part is bitter. Part of you wants to cry, and part of you wants to fight. The tears you cry are hot because they come from your heart, and there is a fire burning in your heart. It's the fire of anger. It's blazing. It's consuming. Its flames leap up under a steaming pot of revenge.

And you are left with a decision. "Do I put the fire out or heat it up? Do I get over it or get even? Do I release it or resent it? Do I let my hurts heal, or do I let hurt turn into hate?"[6]

RESENTMENT AND REVENGE

Resentment is the cocaine of the emotions. It causes our blood to pump and our energy levels to rise.

But, also like cocaine, it demands increasingly larger and more frequent dosages. There is a dangerous point at which anger ceases to be an emotion and becomes a driving force. A person bent on revenge moves unknowingly further and further away from being able to forgive, for to be without the anger is to be without a source of energy.

That explains why the bitter complain to anyone who will listen. They want—they need—to have their fire fanned. That helps explain the existence of the KKK, the skinheads, and other hate organizations. Members of these groups feed each other's anger. And that is why the resentful often appear unreasonable. They are addicted to their bitterness. They don't want to surrender their anger, for to do so would be to surrender their reason to live.

Take bigotry from the racist, and what does he have left? Remove revenge from the heart of the zealot, and her life is empty. Extract chauvinism from the radical sexist, and what remains?

Resentment is like cocaine in another way, too. Cocaine can kill the addict. And anger can kill the angry.

It can kill physically. Chronic anger has been linked with elevated cholesterol, high blood pressure, and other deadly conditions. It can kill emotionally, in that it can raise anxiety levels and lead to depression.[7]

And it can be spiritually fatal, too. It shrivels the soul.

Hatred is the rabid dog that turns on its owner. Revenge is the raging fire that consumes the arsonist. Bitterness is the trap that snares the hunter.

And mercy is the choice that can set them all free.[8]

Let me be very clear. Hatred will sour your outlook and break your back. The load of bitterness is simply too heavy. Your knees will buckle under the strain, and your heart will break beneath the weight. The mountain before you is steep enough without the heaviness of hatred on your back. The wisest choice—the *only* choice—is for you to drop the anger. You will never be called upon to give anyone more grace than God has already given you.[9]

FAILURES

Nothing drags more stubbornly than a sack of failures.

Could you do it all over again, you'd do it differently. You'd be a different person. You'd be more patient. You'd control your tongue. You'd finish what you started. You'd turn the other cheek instead of slapping his. You'd get married first. You wouldn't marry at all. You'd be honest. You'd resist the temptation. You'd run with a different crowd.

But you can't. And as many times as you tell yourself, "What's done is done," what you did can't be undone.

That's part of what Paul meant when he said, "The wages of sin is death" (Rom. 6:23). He didn't say, "The wages of sin is a bad mood." Or, "The wages of sin is a hard day." Nor, "The wages of sin is depression." Read it again. "The wages of sin is death." Sin is fatal.

Can anything be done with it?

Your therapist tells you to talk about it. So you do. You pull the bag into his office and pour the rocks out on his floor and analyze each one. And it's helpful. It feels good to talk, and he's nice. But when the hour is up, you still have to carry the bag out with you.

Your friends tell you not to feel bad. "Everyone slumps a bit in this world," they say. "Not very comforting," you say.

Feel-great-about-life rallies tell you to ignore the thing and be happy! Which works—until you wipe the fog off your mirror and take an honest look. Then you see—it's still there.

Legalists tell you to work the weight off. A candle for every rock. A prayer for every pebble. Sounds logical, but what if I run out of time? Or what if I didn't count correctly? You panic.

What *do* you do with the stones from life's stumbles?[10]

Taking Out
the Trash

She stiffens, steeling herself against the scorn she has learned to expect. As if she needed more shame. Stop him. But how? She awaits his judgment.

But it never comes. His voice is warm and his question honest. "Will you give me your trash?"

Her head draws back. What can he mean?

"Give it to me. Tomorrow. At the landfill. Will you bring it?" He rubs a moist smudge from her cheek with his thumb and stands. "Friday. The landfill."

Long after he leaves, she sits, replaying the scene, retouching her cheek. His voice lingers; his invitation hovers. She tries to dismiss his words but can't. How could he know what he knew? And how could he know and still be so kind? The memory sits on the couch of her soul, an uninvited but welcome guest.

That night's sleep brings her summer dreams. A young girl under blue skies and puffy clouds, playing amid wildflowers, skirt twirling. She dreams of running with hands wide open, brushing the tops of sunflowers. She dreams of happy people filling a meadow with laughter and hope.

But when she wakes, the sky is dark, the clouds billowed, and the streets shadowed. At the foot of her bed lies her sack of trash. Hoisting it over her shoulder, she walks out of the apartment and down the stairs and onto the street, still slushy.

It's Friday.

For a time she stands, thinking. First wondering what he meant, then if he really meant it. She sighs. With hope just barely outweighing hopelessness, she turns toward the edge of town. Others are walking in the same direction. The man beside her smells of alcohol. He's slept many nights in his suit. A teenage girl walks a few feet ahead. The woman of shame hurries to catch up. The girl volunteers an answer before the question can be asked: "Rage. Rage at my father. Rage at my mother. I'm tired of anger. He said he'd take it." She motions to the sack. "I'm going to give it to him."

The woman nods, and the two walk together.[1]

Friday morning. It's trash day. You awake to the roar of the truck, and with pillow-matted hair and your wife's bunny slippers, you dash out to the curb with the week's pickup. The men in the truck have seen it before and can't help but smile. Another last-minute, should-have-done-it-last-night latecomer desperate to rid his garage of last week's smell.

But this morning is different. You missed the truck's wake-up call. Slept right through it. Instead you hear a knock at the door.

"Excuse me, sir. It seems you forgot to put out your trash. Is everything OK?"

The shock of the garbage man's question makes you forget how silly you look in your SpongeBob boxers.

He cares, you think. *He really cares.*

We have a God who makes that request to us every day. He knocks at the door. He sees our cumbersome bags and asks us to give them all to him.

HE SEES YOUR BURDEN

What if our spiritual baggage were visible? Suppose the luggage in our hearts was literal luggage on the street. You know what you'd see most of all? Suitcases of guilt. Bags bulging with binges, blowups, and compromises. Look around you. The fellow in the gray-flannel suit? He's dragging a decade of regrets. The kid with the baggy jeans and nose ring? He'd give anything to retract the words he said to his mother. But he can't. So he tows them along. The woman in the business suit? Looks as if she could run for senator? She'd rather run for help, but she can't run at all. Not hauling that carpetbag of cagmag everywhere she goes.

Listen. The weight of weariness pulls you down. Self-reliance misleads you. Disappointments discourage you. Anxiety plagues you. But guilt? Guilt consumes you.[2]

> Do not be afraid of them. There is nothing concealed that will not be disclosed, or hidden that will not be made known. (Matt. 10:26)

On the surface, those words would seem like a reason for panic rather than a source of peace. Who of us would like to have our secret thoughts made public? Who would want our private sins published? Who would get excited over the idea that every wrong deed we've ever done will be announced to everyone?

You're right; no one would. But we're told over and over that such a thing *will* happen:

Nothing in all creation is hidden from God's sight. Everything is uncovered and laid bare before the eyes of him to whom we must give account. (Heb. 4:13)

He reveals deep and hidden things;
>   he knows what lies in darkness,
>   and light dwells with him. (Dan. 2:22)

But I tell you that men will have to give account on the day of judgment for every careless word they have spoken. (Matt. 12:36)

You have set our iniquities before you,
>   our secret sins in the light of your presence.
>   (Ps. 90:8)

He will bring to light what is hidden in darkness and will expose the motives of men's hearts.
(1 Cor. 4:5)

To think of the disclosure of my hidden heart conjures up emotions of shame, humiliation, and embarrassment in me. There are things I've done that I want no one to know. There are thoughts

I've thought I would never want to be revealed. So why does Jesus point to the day of revelation as a reason for *courage?* How can I take strength in what should be a moment of anguish?

The answer is found in Romans 2:16. Let out a sigh of relief as you underline the last three words: "This will take place on the day when God will judge men's secrets *through Jesus Christ.*"

Did you see it? Jesus is the screen through which God looks when he judges our sins. Now read another chorus of verses and focus on their promise:

Therefore, there is now no condemnation for those who are in Christ Jesus. (Rom. 8:1)

[God] justifies those who have faith in Jesus. (Rom. 3:26)

Through him everyone who believes is justified from everything. (Acts 13:39)

For I will forgive their wickedness
    and will remember their sins no more.
    (Heb. 8:12)

For you died, and your life is now hidden with Christ in God. (Col. 3:3)

If you are in Christ, these promises are not only a source of joy. They are also the foundations of true courage. You are guaranteed that your sins will be filtered through, hidden in, and screened out by the sacrifice of Jesus. When God looks at you, he doesn't see you; he sees the One who surrounds you. That means that failure is not a concern for you. Your victory is secure. How could you not be courageous?[3]

HE WANTS YOUR BURDEN

Come to me, all you who are weary and burdened, and I will give you rest. (Matt. 11:28)

Come to me. . . . The invitation is to come to him. Why him?

He offered the invitation as a penniless rabbi in an oppressed nation. He had no political office, no connections with the authorities in Rome. He hadn't written a bestseller or earned a diploma.

Yet, he dared to look at the leathery faces of farmers and tired faces of housewives and offer rest. He looked into the disillusioned eyes of a preacher or two from Jerusalem. He gazed at the cynical stare of a banker and the hungry eyes of a bartender and made this paradoxical promise: "Take my yoke upon you and learn from me, for I am gentle and humble in heart, and you will find rest for your souls" (Matt. 11:29).

The people came. They came out of the cul-de-sacs and office complexes of their day. They brought him the burdens of their existence, and he gave them not religion, not doctrine, not systems, but rest.

As a result, they called him Lord.

As a result, they called him Savior.

Not so much because of what he said, but because of what he did.

What he did on the cross during six hours, one Friday.[4]

When we surrender to God our cumbersome sacks, we don't just give up something; we gain something. God replaces them with a lightweight, tailor-made, sorrow-resistant attaché of gratitude.

What will you gain with gratitude? You may gain your marriage. You may gain precious hours with your children. You may gain your self-respect. You may gain joy.[5]

Good
Riddance

The landfill is tall with trash—papers and broken brooms and old beds and rusty cars. By the time they reach the hill, the line to the top is long. Hundreds walk ahead of them. All wait in silence, stunned by what they hear—a scream, a pain-pierced roar that hangs in the air for moments, interrupted only by a groan. Then the scream again.

His.

As they draw nearer, they know why. He kneels before each, gesturing toward the sack, offering a request, then a prayer. "May I have it? And may you never feel it again." Then he bows his head and lifts the sack, emptying its contents upon himself. The selfishness of the glutton, the bitterness of the angry, the possessiveness of the insecure. He feels what they felt. It is as if he'd lied or cheated or cursed his Maker.

Upon her turn, the woman pauses. Hesitates. His eyes compel her to step forward. He reaches for her trash and takes it from her. "You can't live with this," he explains. "You weren't made to." With head down, he empties her shame *upon his shoulders. Then looking toward the heavens with tear-flooded eyes, he screams, "I'm sorry!"*

"But you did nothing!" she cries.

Still, he sobs as she has sobbed into her pillow a hundred nights. That's when she realizes that his cry is hers. Her shame his.

With her thumb she touches his cheek, and for the first step in a long nighttime, she has no trash to carry.

With the others she stands at the base of the hill and watches as he is buried under a mound of misery. For some time he moans. Then nothing. Just silence.[1]

Everyone in the house always seems to walk by the garbage can. Doesn't anybody see the four-foot-high stack of newspapers? The banana peels on the table? The coffee grounds sprinkled on the linoleum?

Denial does not remove the trash. Admitting that there is trash is the first step toward disposal.

If we confess our sins, he is faithful and just to forgive us our sins, and to cleanse us from all unrighteousness. (1 John 1:9 KJV)

Do you want to say good riddance to the trash bags in your life? First John 1:9 tells you how. Confession leads to forgiveness, and forgiveness leads to cleansing.

CONFESSION

Confession does not create a relationship with God; it simply nourishes it. If you are a believer, admission of sins does not alter your position before God, but it does enhance your peace with God. When you confess, you agree; you quit arguing with God and agree with him about your sin. Unconfessed sin leads to a state of disagreement. You may be God's child, but you don't want to talk to him. He still loves you, but until you admit what you've done, there's going to be tension in the house.

But just as unconfessed sin hinders joy, confessed sin releases it.[2]

Confession does for the soul what preparing the land does for the field. Before the farmer sows the seed, he works the acreage, removing the rocks and pulling the stumps. He knows that seed grows better if the land is prepared. Confession is the act of inviting God to walk the acreage of our hearts. "There is a rock of greed over here, Father. I can't budge it. And that tree of guilt near the fence? Its roots are long and deep. And may I show you some dry soil too crusty for seed?" God's seed grows better if the soil of the heart is cleared.

And so the Father and the Son walk the field together, digging and pulling, preparing the heart for fruit. Confession invites the Father to work the soil of the soul.

Confession seeks pardon from God, not amnesty. Pardon presumes guilt; amnesty, derived from the same Greek word as *amnesia,* "forgets" the alleged offense without imputing guilt. Confession admits wrong and seeks forgiveness; amnesty denies wrong and claims innocence.[3]

FORGIVENESS

Come with me to the hill of Calvary.

Watch as the soldiers shove the Carpenter to

the ground and stretch his arms against the beams. One presses a knee against a forearm and a spike against a hand. Jesus turns his face toward the nail just as the soldier lifts the hammer to strike it.

Couldn't Jesus have stopped him? With a flex of the biceps, with a clench of the fist, he could have resisted. Is this not the same hand that stilled the sea? Cleansed the Temple? Summoned the dead?

But the fist doesn't clench . . . and the moment isn't aborted. . . .

The crowd at the cross concluded that the purpose of the pounding was to skewer the hands of Christ to a beam. But they were only half-right. We can't fault them for missing the other half. They couldn't see it. But Jesus could. And heaven could. And we can.

Through the eyes of Scripture we see what others missed but what Jesus saw. "He canceled the record that contained the charges against us. He took it and destroyed it by nailing it to Christ's cross" (Col. 2:14 NLT).

Between Jesus' hand and the wood there was a

list. A long list. A list of our mistakes: our lusts and lies and greedy moments and prodigal years. A list of our sins.

Dangling from the cross was an itemized catalog of your sins. The bad decisions from last year. The bad attitudes from last week. There, in broad daylight for all of heaven to see, was a list of your mistakes.

God had penned a list of our faults. The list God had made, however, cannot be read. The words can't be deciphered. The mistakes are covered. The sins are hidden. Those at the top are hidden by his hand; those down the list are covered by his blood. Your sins are "blotted out" by Jesus (Isa. 44:22 KJV). "He has forgiven you all your sins: he has utterly wiped out the written evidence of broken commandments which always hung over our heads, and has completely annulled it by nailing it to the cross" (Col. 2:13–14 PHILLIPS).

What kept Jesus from resisting? This warrant, this tabulation of your failures. He knew the price of those sins was death. He knew the source of those sins was you, and since he couldn't bear the thought of eternity without you, he chose the nails.

The hand squeezing the handle was not a Roman infantryman.

The force behind the hammer was not an angry mob.

The verdict behind the death was not decided by jealous Jews.

Jesus himself chose the nails.

So the hands of Jesus opened up. Had the soldier hesitated, Jesus himself would have swung the mallet. He knew how; he was no stranger to the driving of nails. As a carpenter he knew what it took. And as a Savior he knew what it meant. He knew that the purpose of the nail was to place your sins where they could be hidden by his sacrifice and covered by his blood.

So Jesus himself swung the hammer.

The same hand that stilled the seas stills your guilt.

The same hand that cleansed the Temple cleanses your heart.

The hand is the hand of God.

The nail is the nail of God.

And as the hands of Jesus opened for the nail, the doors of heaven opened for you.[4]

CLEANSING

God does more than forgive our mistakes; he removes them! We simply have to take them to him.

He not only wants the mistakes we've made. He wants the ones we are making! Are you making some? Are you drinking too much? Are you cheating at work or cheating at marriage? Are you mismanaging money? Are you mismanaging your life?

If so, don't pretend nothing is wrong. Don't pretend you don't fall. Don't try to get back in the game. Go first to God. The first step after a stumble must be in the direction of the cross. "If we confess our sins to God, he can always be trusted to forgive us and take our sins away" (1 John 1:9 CEV).

What can you leave at the cross?[5]

Thousands of years before Jesus was called the Lamb of God, God promised forgiveness.

"Someday," he promised Jeremiah, "someday I will remember their sins no more."

"Someday," God confided to Hosea, "these people will be my people, and I will be their God."

"And someday," wrote David, "the mistakes of men will be tossed, not under a rug or behind the sofa, but far, far away. As far as the east is from the west."

And do you know what? That someday came. On a garbage heap outside of Jerusalem.

Someday the almighty God, who has every right to make me burn forever, will look past my apathy, my gluttony, my lying, and my lusting. He will point to the cross and invite me to come home . . . forgiven . . . forever.[6]

A New Beginning

The people sit among the wrecked cars and papers and discarded stoves and wonder who this man is and what he has done. Like mourners at a wake, they linger. Some share stories. Others say nothing. All cast occasional glances at the landfill. It feels odd, loitering near the heap. But it feels even stranger to think of leaving.

So they stay. Through the night and into the next day. Darkness comes again. A kinship connects them, a kinship through the trashman. Some doze. Others build fires in the metal drums and speak of the sudden abundance of stars in the night sky. By early morning most are asleep.

They almost miss the moment. It is the young girl who sees it. The girl with the rage. She doesn't trust her eyes at first, but when she looks again, she knows.

Her words are soft, intended for no one. "He's standing."

Then aloud, for her friend, "He's standing."

And louder for all, "He's standing!"

She turns; all turn. They see him silhouetted against a golden sun.

Standing. Indeed.[^1]

47

The story began with cumbersome trash bags in hand and closed with a trashman covered in rubbish. It all seemed to end there, as he lay buried under the slop and mess. The people are free, and the trashman is dead. Fade to black. Roll credits.

But suddenly the trashman rises. Standing tall. Himself unencumbered. Free.

Now a new story begins. This time with a risen Savior and a group of followers who are sinless. He has shown his power. He can be trusted. We can live free . . . forever.

FREEDOM

We are waiting for God to finish making us his own children, which means our bodies will be made free. (Rom. 8:23 NCV)

Are our bodies now free? No. Paul describes them as our "earthy bodies" (Phil. 3:21 MSG). Or as other translations state:

"our lowly body" (NKJV)

"the body of our humble state" (NASB)

"these weak mortal bodies" (NLT)

"our vile body" (KJV)

"our simple bodies" (NCV)

You could add your own adjective, couldn't you? Which word describes your body? My *cancerous* body? My *arthritic* body? My *deformed* body? My *crippled* body? My *addicted* body? My *ever-expanding* body? The word may be different, but the message is the same: These bodies are weak. They began decaying the minute we began breathing.

And, according to God, that's a part of the plan. Every wrinkle and every needle take us one step closer to the last step when Jesus will change our simple bodies into forever bodies. No pain. No depression. No sickness. No end.

This is not our forever house. It will serve for the time being. But there is nothing like the moment we enter his door.

Molly can tell you. After a month in our house she ran away. I came home one night to find the place unusually quiet. Molly was gone.

She'd slipped out unnoticed. The search began immediately. Within an hour we knew that she was far, far from home. Now, if you don't like pets, what I'm about to say is going to sound strange. If you do like pets, you will understand.

You'll understand why we walked up and down the street calling her name. You'll understand why I drove around the neighborhood at 10:30 P.M. You'll understand why I put up a poster in the convenience store and convened the family for a prayer. (Honestly, I did.) You'll understand why I sent e-mails to the staff, asking for prayers, and to her breeder, asking for advice. And you'll understand why we were ready to toss the confetti and party when she showed up.

Here is what happened. The next morning Denalyn was on her way home from taking the girls to school when she saw the trash truck. She asked the workers to keep an eye out for Molly and then hurried home to host a moms' prayer group. Soon after the ladies arrived, the trash truck pulled into our driveway, a worker opened the door, and out bounded our dog. She had been found.

When Denalyn called to tell me the news, I could barely hear her voice. It was Mardi Gras in the kitchen. The ladies were celebrating the return of Molly.

This story pops with symbolism. The master leaving his house, searching for the lost. Victories in the midst of prayer. Great things coming out of trash. But most of all: the celebration at the coming home. That's something else you have in common with Molly—a party at your home-coming.

By that moment only one bag will remain. Not guilt. It was dropped at Calvary. Not the fear of death. It was left at the grave. The only lingering luggage will be this God-given longing for home. And when you see him, you'll set it down. Just as a returning soldier drops his duffel when he sees his wife, you'll drop your longing when you see your Father. Those you love will shout. Those you know will applaud. But all the noise will cease when he cups your chin and says, "Welcome home." And with scarred hand he'll wipe every tear from your eye. And you will dwell in the house of your Lord—forever.[2]

TAKE OUT YOUR TRASH

Come to me, all you who are weary and burdened, and I will give you rest. (Matt. 11:28)

What was Jesus thinking when he made this comment? Was he offering a clichéd response to someone's need? "Hey, whatever I can do. Give me a call."

Was he kidding?

Or was he serious?

Jesus appeals to us to bring him those things that burden us and weigh us down. We weren't made to live with sin but designed to live free. We think we can do it for a time, then realize it's just too heavy. The weight of our sins, our failures, and our worries is too much for one person to carry alone.

Jesus wants them all.

During this simple prayer, it's time to take your bags to the street. It's Friday morning. Trash day. And soon, it will all be gone.

A New Beginning

Dear Jesus,

I have been carrying around sacks of shame, worry, pain, resentment, and failure for too long. I have tried to live with the guilt and hurt, but they've grown heavy. My arms ache. My heart grieves. I can't move forward any longer.

I realize that freedom begins not only by confessing my sin but by giving it to you. Once my sins are released from me to you, then you take my burden to the cross and there dispose of it. Forever.

I once carried failure, but now I have forgiveness.

I once carried hate, but now I have hope.

I once carried fear, but now I have freedom.

Thank you for removing the garbage of my life. No longer is my life the same ol' story. Now there is a new beginning. I am free because it is all in your hands.

Amen

NOTES

CARRYING THE WEIGHT

1. Max Lucado, *Next Door Savior* (Nashville: W Publishing Group, 2003), 73.

2. Jerry Schwartz, "Where Does One Stash That Trash Ash?" *San Antonio Express News,* 3 September 2000, sec. 29A.

3. You can read about Cain in Genesis 4:1–8; Martha in Luke 10:38–42; and the Pharisees in Matthew 12:1–14.

4. Max Lucado, *A Love Worth Giving: Living in the Overflow of God's Love* (Nashville: W Publishing Group, 2002), 87–89, 94.

Notes

WHAT'S INSIDE THE BAGS?

1. Lucado, *Next Door Savior,* 73–74.

2. Madeleine Blais, "Who's Going to Love Judy Bucknell?" (Part 1), *Miami Herald,* 12 October 1980, Tropic Magazine.

3. Blais, "Judy Bucknell."

4. Max Lucado, *No Wonder They Call Him the Savior* (Portland, Oreg.: Multnomah Press, 1986), 44–45.

5. Max Lucado, *Traveling Light: Releasing the Burdens You Were Never Intended to Bear* (Nashville: W Publishing Group, 2001), 47–48.

6. Max Lucado, *The Applause of Heaven* (Dallas: Word Publishing, 1990), 108.

7. Archibald D. Hart, *The Hidden Link Between Adrenaline and Stress* (Waco, Tex.: Word, 1986), 101, 142–45.

8. Lucado, *The Applause of Heaven,* 111–12.

9. Max Lucado, *In the Grip of Grace* (Dallas: Word Publishing, 1996), 156–57.

10. Max Lucado, *Six Hours, One Friday: Anchoring to the Cross* (Portland, Oreg.: Multnomah Press, 1989), 83–84.

TAKING OUT THE TRASH

1. Lucado, *Next Door Savior,* 74–75.

2. Lucado, *Traveling Light,* 66.

3. Lucado, *The Applause of Heaven,* 83–85.

4. Lucado, *Six Hours, One Friday,* 32–33.

5. Lucado, *Traveling Light,* 34.

GOOD RIDDANCE

1. Lucado, *Next Door Savior,* 75–76.

2. Max Lucado, *The Great House of God: A Home for Your Heart* (Dallas: Word Publishing, 1997), 125.

3. Lucado, *In the Grip of Grace,* 122.

4. Max Lucado, *He Chose the Nails: What God Did to Win Your Heart* (Nashville: Word Publishing, 2000), 32, 33–35.

5. Lucado, *He Chose the Nails,* 141.

6. Max Lucado, *On the Anvil* (Wheaton, Ill.: Tyndale House Publishers, 1985), 85.

Notes

A NEW BEGINNING

1. Lucado, *Next Door Savior*, 76.

2. Lucado, *Traveling Light*, 155–57.